Hedgehogs

Nocturnal Foragers

Rebecca Rissman

Heinemann
LIBRARY
Chicago, Illinois

Edited by Brynn Baker, Clare Lewis, and
    Helen Cox Cannons
Designed by Kyle Grenz and Tim Bond
Picture research by Tracy Cummins
Production by Helen McCreath
Originated by Capstone Global Library Ltd
Printed and bound in China by Leo Paper Group

18 17 16 15 14
10 9 8 7 6 5 4 3 2 1

**Library of Congress Cataloging-in-Publication
Data**

ISBN 978-1-4846-0313-0 (hardcover)
ISBN 978-1-4846-0319-2 (paperback)
ISBN 978-1-4846-0331-4 (eBook PDF)

Acknowledgments

We would like to thank the following for permission
to reproduce photographs: Alamy: © blickwinkel, 22,
© FLPA, 9, 23b, © incamerastock, 4, 23d, © Juniors
Bildarchiv GmbH, 15, © Nature Picture Library, 5, 23e,
© Roger Allen Photography, 17, © Shaun Finch - Coy-
ote-Photography.co.uk, 21; FLPA: Derek Middleton, 7
mouse, Imagebroker, 7 owl, Michael Durham/Minden
Pictures, 7 bat, Paul Hobson, 12, 23f, Roger Tidman, 18,
Wayne Hutchinson, 11, 23g; Photoshot: TIPS/bruno de
faveri, front cover;
Shutterstock: albinoni, 16, Andrew Astbury, 7 fox, Cre-
ativeNature.nl, 6, back cover, D. Kucharski K. Kucharska,
10, Jiri Vaclavek, 14, 23c, Monkey Business Images, 20,
Smokedsalmon, 19, 23a, Vishnevskiy Vasily, 13

Every effort has been made to contact copyright holders
of material reproduced in this book. Any omissions will
be rectified in subsequent printings if notice is given to
the publisher.

Contents

What Is a Hedgehog?

A hedgehog is a small **mammal**.

It has a round body covered in sharp brown or gray spines.

A hedgehog has four short legs with sharp claws for digging and catching **prey**.

You rarely see hedgehogs during the day. This is because they are **nocturnal**.

What Does Nocturnal Mean?

Nocturnal means awake during the night.

Animals that are nocturnal sleep during the day.

Many different animals are nocturnal.

Bats, owls, foxes, and mice are nocturnal.

Where Do Hedgehogs Live?

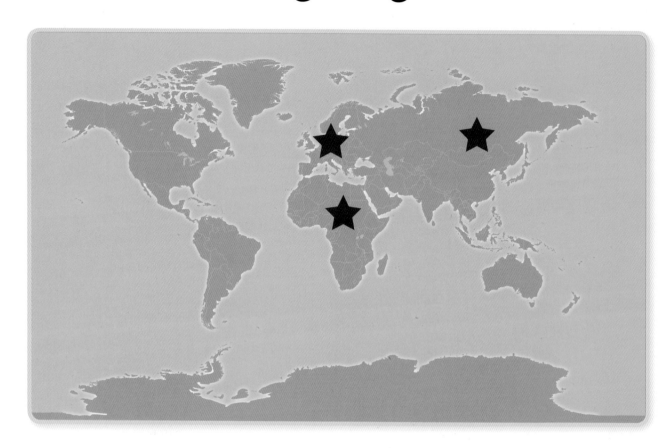

Most wild hedgehogs live in Europe, Asia, and Africa.

Hedgehogs can be found in forests, fields, and farmlands.

Hedgehogs can also be found in neighborhood parks and gardens.

Hedgehogs often hide in bushes.

What Do Hedgehogs Eat?

Hedgehogs search for food along bushes and near the roots of other plants.

They eat insects, worms, centipedes, and small animals, such as mice.

Some people think hedgehogs got their name because of the noises they make.

Hedgehogs make a grunting noise like a hog or pig when they hunt for food.

Do Hedgehogs Have Predators?

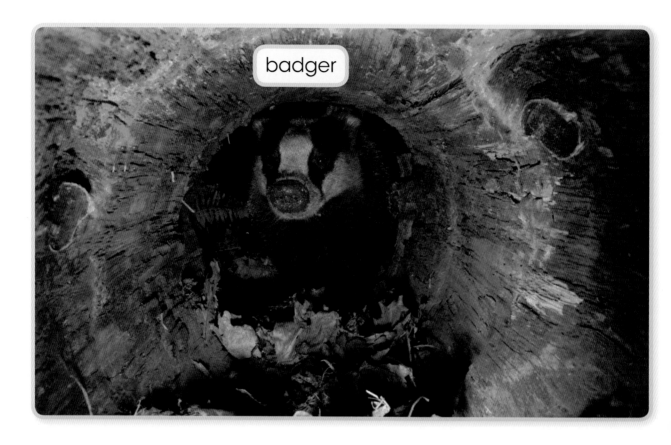

badger

Some animals hunt hedgehogs for food.

Badgers, owls, and foxes are hedgehog **predators**.

When a predator is nearby, a hedgehog rolls into a sharp, spiny ball.

This scares predators away!

What Are Hedgehog Babies Like?

Mother hedgehogs give birth to one or two **litters** of babies each year.

Hedgehog litters usually have four to five babies.

Hedgehog babies' spines are soft and very short when they are born.

After only two weeks, the young hedgehogs grow a full covering of spines.

Where Do Hedgehogs Go in Winter?

Hedgehogs that live in cold places hibernate during winter.

To hibernate means to sleep or rest in a safe place all through winter.

Hedgehogs hibernate in nests made of sticks, leaves, and grass.

Some hedgehogs even move into different nests in the middle of winter.

How Can You Spot Hedgehogs?

During the day, look for signs that hedgehogs have been nearby.

Hedgehog droppings are black and only as long as a penny.

Hedgehogs are easiest to spot at **dusk** or just after **dawn**.

If you are looking for a hedgehog in the dark, listen for grunts and squeals.

How Can You Help Hedgehogs?

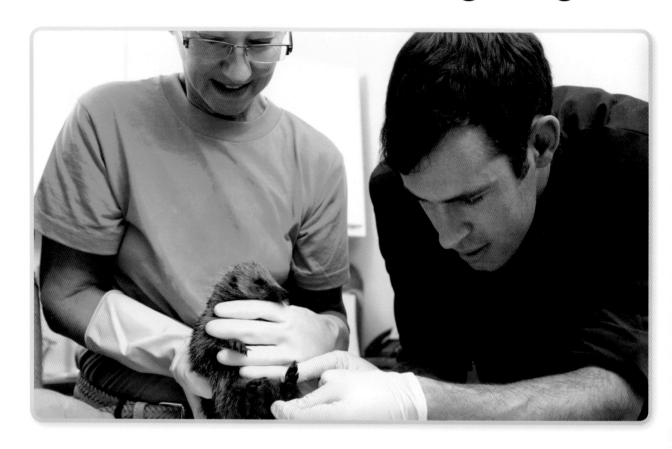

Hedgehogs that come out during the day are usually sick.

If you see a hedgehog during the day, ask a trusted adult to call a veterinarian.

Hedgehogs can get hurt when people light bonfires.

Have adults check that there are no hedgehogs hiding in the wood before they light bonfires.

Hedgehog Body Map

spine

eye

claw

Picture Glossary

 **dawn** time of day when the sun first rises

 **dusk** time of day when the sun sets

 **litter** group of baby animals born from the same mother at the same time

 **mammal** warm-blooded animal that has a backbone, hair or fur, and gives birth to live babies that feed on milk from their mother

 **nocturnal** awake at night and asleep during the day

 **predator** animal that hunts other animals for food

 **prey** animal that is hunted by other animals

Find Out More

Books

Dunn, Mary R. *Hedgehogs.* Nocturnal Animals. Mankato, Minn.: Capstone Press, 2011.

Vanderlip, Sharon. *Hedgehogs: Everything about Purchase, Care, and Nutrition.* A Complete Pet Owner's Manual. Haupauge, NY: Barron's, 2010

Websites

Discover more nocturnal animals at:
http://bbc.co.uk/nature/adaptations/Nocturnality

Learn more about hedgehogs at:
http://kids.nationalgeographic.com/kids/animals/creaturefeature/hedgehog

Index